Text by
ROMEO CIANCHETTA

D1330606

THE ILLUSTRATED LIFE OF ST. FRANCIS

Fifty antique watercolors on the life of the Saint by P. Subercaseaux

Edited by LITOVALD - Valdagno
Distributed by DACA - Assisi

We would like to try to convey to the reader the surprise and enthusiasm experienced by anyone who, while rummaging through old publications at a sidewalk antiques stall, happened to run across the watercolors done by Subercaseaux, illustrating prominent episodes in the life of St Francis. Although this collection, which was published in a slim volume in 1910, was successful, all further traces of it were lost.

Subercaseaux follows in the wake of the late eighteenth-century Romantic movement, with its graphic simplicity, expressive candor, intensity of feeling and emotional participation.

Perhaps it is daring of us to republish these poetic little paintings, but we wanted to join the stream of artists who are attempting to lend renewed value to turn-of-the-century expressive sincerity, which was suffused with a streak of ingenuity. Although these works do have an almost cartoon-like first-edition quality, they nevertheless fit in fully with the spirit of the times. More importantly, however, the emotions expressed here have not undergone any radical changes over the years, for love, serenity, tenderness and religiousness are still harbored within modern man.

The episodes depicted by the artist are the ones recounted by the Saint's early biographers, Thomas of Celano, St Bonaventure and the anonymous author of The Little Flowers.

Assisi   Mauceni 2001

ILLUSTRATIONS

THE BIRTH OF ST FRANCIS

St Francis was born in Assisi in 1183, the son of Monna Pica and Peter Bernardone. Legend has it that Monna Pica gave birth to her first-born in a stall near their house, following the instructions given to her by a mysterious pilgrim who had come to her door before the birth. Perhaps this legend arose to strengthen the parallels drawn between the life of Christ

and the life of Francis. At the baptismal font in the Cathedral of San Rufino, he was given the name of John, but upon his return from a business trip to France, his father later changed it to Francis to commemorate the land that had made him wealthy.

MONNA PICA

Monna Pica, Francis' mother, was of Provençal origin and, since the first tender and loving words heard by little Francis were in French, this language held a special place in his heart. In fact, according to his first biographer, Thomas of Celano, whenever he wanted to express his joy, he sang in the lilting tongue of the troubadours of chivalrous Provence.

Like all mothers, Pica dreamed that her son would be destined for glory. Nevertheless, she did not reproach or oppose him in his spiritual change and in fact, she secretly helped him. Going against the wishes of her husband, Peter Bernardone, she freed Francis from the nook under the stairs, where his father hand imprisoned him in chains.

HE ASKS A BEGGAR FOR FORGIVENESS

Francis, who was intently negotiating over a bolt of cloth in his father's store, refused to pay any attention to a beggar who had asked him for alms in God's name. He was undoubtedly just distracted for a moment, since he had never sent a poor man away empty-handed. He suddenly left the customer and ran after the beggar. After asking the man for forgiveness, he gave him a generous amount of money.

THE ENCHANTMENT OF YOUTH

Young Francis, who had plenty of money and was highly intelligent, and who was also friendly, boastful, well-dressed and generous, was spontaneously elected "prince of the Assisi youth brigade."

Since he was most popular at banquets, first in poetry contests and first in the youth activities of his day, he also thought he would excel at the art of war. He was a valorous knight during the war against Perugia and then left for Apulia to defend the imperial rights of Constance, the widow of Henry IV.

Francis was "an object of wonder to everyone and, with pompous vanity, he strived to beat everyone at games, in elegance, with fine witticisms, in song and in his luxurious and flowing robes: he was not stingy but prodigal, and was not avid but spendthrift" (1 Cel 2).

FRANCIS RECOVERS

The young man, exhausted by his long illness, began to think about things differently than usual. To regain his strength, he had to use a cane to lean on, and one day he went out and began to look more closely at the countryside spread out around him, at the beauty of the fields and the amenities of the vineyards, but everything that was a delight to the eye was no longer enjoyable to him. He was amazed by this sudden change and considered foolish those whose hearts were attached to goods of this kind (1 Cel 2).

GOING OFF TO WAR

In 1202, a bitter conflict arose between Assisi and Perugia. Assisi, which was already a free commune, had exiled the feudal lords who had long antagonized the city. Perugia hosted and protected them and requested that they be allowed to return. When Assisi refused, a war broke out between the two cities. Twenty-year-old Francis joined the city militia as a horseman. During the battle of Collestrada, a district of Perugia, he was made prisoner and was conducted to the Perugia prison of Sopramura, where he remained for almost a year. While prison life was harsh, Francis distinguished himself nevertheless. He was generous and lively, he lavished his attentions on his companions and, with his songs, he kept up their hopes for freedom.

A WARNING FROM HEAVEN

After a sleepless night, Francis was ready and, impatient and full of life, he took up the shield of faith, donning the arms of deep faith to fight the Lord's battles. He went through the streets of the city while, in his divine enthusiasm, he accused himself of being lazy and base (1 Cel 5).

LADY POVERTY

After his return from Spoleto, Francis meditated over the crystal clear voice that, in his dream, had ordered him to return to Assisi to await further orders. This waiting period had a profound effect on his spirit and provoked a change in his daily habits: he sought solitude and prayer. He wanted to cut his ties with the past and invited his friends to a "farewell dinner". His companions, unaware of Francis' true intentions, came in a festive mood, certain that, given the well-known extravagance of the prince of their brigade, Francis would offer an unforgettable party. He went wearing precious and luxurious clothes and, as a distinguishing mark of "the prince of parties", carried a "walking stick decorated with multicolored ribbons". Succulent dishes, song, good cheer, toasts and exhuberant joy marked the course of their banquet. Towards the end of the supper, Francis silently slipped out of the room without fanfare and disappeared.

As soon as his friends realized this, they went to look for him. They found him standing in a square, gazing at the sky in rapture. They shook him and, at their insistent questioning, he candidly responded that "he was dreaming of the face of his bride to be, Lady Poverty.

AT THE APOSTLE'S SEPULCHER

As a teenager, he went on a pilgrimage to the tomb of St Peter in Rome. When he saw that the pilgrims threw just a few coins on the apostle's tomb as alms, he marveled at their stinginess and, with a rush of generosity that was typical of him, he threw down all his money without keeping

anything for his return trip to Assisi. Then he exchanged his princely clothing for the clothes of a beggar and took the man's place, holding his arm outstretched for alms. This was a gesture of love towards the poor and of conscious personal humiliation.

FRANCIS EMBRACES THE LEPER

After the dream he had in Spoleto in which he heard a divine voice enjoining him to return to Assisi to receive further orders, Francis became seriously ill. While he was recovering, he rode on horseback towards a leper hospice located not far from the Portiuncola. He met a leper along the way, but feeling repulsed by him, Francis wanted to flee.... Instead, he jumped down from his horse, went up the leper and embraced him. This was his greatest victory and it marked the turning point in his life. In the testament he dictated before he died, he declared, "everything that had seemed bitter to me was turned into sweetness of the soul and body".

ST FRANCIS PRAYS BEFORE THE CRUCIFIX OF SAN DAMIANO

"Returning from Spoleto to Assisi, one day when he had gone out to meditate in the countryside, he found himself near the little church of San Damiano, which was falling into ruin because it was so old. Inspired by God, he went in.

"At the foot of the Crucifix, he prayed with intense fervor and his soul was filled with joy. Then he turned his tearful eyes upward and heard a mysterious voice in his ears. That voice was coming down from the lips of the crucified Christ, and they were addressed to him. It said to him three times, 'Francis, repair my house which, as you can see, is in ruins'" (Bon II, 1).

This was a symbolic order that encharged Francis with a very lofty task: he was to restore the divine principles of the Church of Christ, which was threatened by heresy, immorality and simony. Francis was unable to grasp the hidden meaning behind this task and could only understand its literal significance.

RESTORATION OF SAN DAMIANO

Francis had interpreted the instructions given to him by the Crucifix of San Damiano in a literal sense: "Go, Francis, and restore my house that is in ruins". In order to obtain the money required to repair the little church, he took some bolts of precious fabric from his father's warehouse, went to Foligno and sold the cloth, as well as his horse.

He offered the money he earned to the custodian of the church so that the work could be done, but the custodian refused to accept the funds since he believed they were ill-gotten gains and feared the wrath of Fran-

cis' father, Peter Bernardone.

Indeed, several days later, Francis' father called him forth to be judged by Bishop Guido.

Francis took off all his clothes and, as he give them back to his father, he renounced his inheritance, exclaiming, "Hear me, all of you: until now, I recognized Peter Bernardone as my father. From now on, I can freely say Our Father who art in Heaven!"

THE FOLLY OF THE CROSS

No, the people of Assisi refused to accept that Francis, the son of rich Peter Bernardone — the one-time frivolous, boastful and generous prince of the youth brigades — could suddenly have chosen a life of poverty, humiliation and begging. Only a madman would exchange wealth for poverty, admiration for derision, "luxurious and flowing robes" for a miserably torn and patched-up tunic. Whenever he walked through the city streets, everyone called him "foolish and crazy" and threw rocks and mud at him. Francis didn't get angry and instead, he joyfully accepted their insults, thanking the Lord for his trials. He would simply bless his persecutors and forgive them.

Standing in the squares and church courtyards, he preached penance, peace and the reign of God. Initially, his fellow citizens approached him diffidently, out of curiosity, but then rushed to him in ever growing numbers. Nobles and commoners, clerics and laymen — everyone listened to him in admiration and was edified by him.

ON THE ROAD TO GUBBIO
THE SERVANT OF THE MONASTERY

After renouncing all property, Francis was free of all ties. Barefoot and wearing only the sack given to him by the Bishop's gardener to cover his nakedness, he started off on foot towards Gubbio, singing and proclaiming himself "the herald of the Great King". He asked the Benedictines of St Mary's of Valfabbrica for hospitality and stayed there for several days, working as a kitchen hand. Then he left again for Gubbio, where he was

welcomed by his comrade in arms, the knight Frederic Spadalunga, who, as legend has it, dressed him in the tunic that was to become the Franciscan habit (a cross-shaped cowl).

He preached the Gospel throughout the snow-covered streets of the city, and when he returned to Assisi in the spring, he completed the restoration work on the Church of San Damiano.

TO THE LEPER HOSPITAL

As soon as he finished work to restore the little church of San Damiano and was done preaching the Gospel, he would rush to the leper hospital. He washed them, dressed their sores, embraced them and comforted them, lighting their souls with the hope that they would be cured.

THE BEGGAR

After he had given up his father's property before Bishop Guido, Francis, whom all his fellows citizens had known as the son of the rich merchant, Peter Bernardone, and who had been considered the most brilliant, elegant, wealthy and generous of all the young men of Assisi, humbled himself by begging for table scraps from door to door. He rejoiced when he received these leftovers, graciously thanking his benefactors by blessing them, and then ate disgusting watery soup and stale scraps of bread as if they were precious gifts of the Lord.

PREACHING THE GOSPEL AND PENANCE

The people of Assisi, who were initially hostile towards him, followed Francis' public manifestations with ill-concealed curiosity. They began to respond to his cheerful greeting of "peace and all good" and listened to his sermons in increasingly larger groups. His message, proclaimed in a clear, steady and convincing voice, found its way into the hearts of his listeners and stirred their admiration. Bernard of Quintavalle, a rich and aristocratic young man, approached him and invited him to his patrician palace. During the night, Francis, thinking that Bernard had fallen asleep, jumped out of bed and began to pray. Instead, Bernard was listening to

his dialogue with the Lord and was deeply moved by it. He too got up, went over to Francis and joined him in prayer. The next morning, they went to the Church of St Nicolò, opened the Gospel at random and read the passage, "If you wish to be perfect, go, sell everything you have and give it to the poor" (Matthew). Bernard sold all his possessions, donated them to the poor and asked Francis to accept him as his first companion.

A WELCOME DISCIPLE

Giles, a farmer's son, avidly listened to accounts of Francis' sermons. He knew that Bernard of Quintavalle and Peter Catanii, men who were very well-known in Assisi due to their social status, had become his companions in penance and prayer at the little church of the Portiuncola. As Brother Leo tells us, "Deep down, he had decided to become Francis' third companion. He was not familiar with the place so he asked God to lead him down the right road. And there came blessed Francis, who was going to pray in the woods nearby. When he saw him, Giles rejoiced and threw himself at his feet. Francis asked him, 'What do you want?' and he replied 'I want to go with you.'

"Francis lifted him up with his hand, led him to the little church and called Brother Bernard, saying to him, 'The Lord has sent us a good brother. Let us welcome him'."

THE FIRST MISSION
Once Pope Innocent III had granted his authorization to preach the Gospel, Francis sent his first companions in pairs on religious missions along the roads of Italy and Europe.

THE VOCATION OF ANGELO TANCREDI

The noble knight, Angelo Tancredi of Assisi, asked if he could become part of the community of the Portiuncola. This was a highly significant testimonial, for it meant that Francis' preaching had broken through the pride of the feudal lord and through the revolutionary spirit of the people, to the point that through Francis' mediation, a peace treaty was reached between the aristocratic *majores* class and the *minores* in Assisi.

THE TRIP TO ROME

When his followers numbered twelve, Francis felt it was necessary to obtain from the Pope the Rule of Life, which was based on poverty and permission to preach. During the month of September, he set out with them from Rivotorto, where he had created an initial tiny convent known as

the "Hovel" and went to Rome.
After a lengthy wait, Pope Innocent III received him and orally approved
the Rule, after overcoming some initial doubts he had had concerning the
excessive severity of the regulation imposing the observance of utter
poverty.

OTTO IV PASSES NEAR THE HOVEL

During the fall of 1209, not far from the hovel in Rivotorto, "the Emperor Otto was passing through the place with clamor and pomp to be crowned by the Pope. The most holy father, Francis, who was living with his brothers in that hovel, did not even go out to watch, and he would not let anyone else do so except one who continuously called to the emperor that his reign would last but a short time" (I Cel., 43). The prophecy later came true.

CLARE

Clare, daughter of the nobleman Favarone di Offreduccio, a young woman of exemplary virtue, listened to Francis' sermons with admiration and devotion. She wanted to meet him so that she could leave worldly vainglory behind and offer her life to Jesus Christ, the great King.

Accompanied by her relative Bona di Guelfuccio so that "that divine attraction would not be misinterpreted", the young girl left her family palace and secretly made her way to the man of God, whose words seemed like flames to her and whose works seemed divine.

CLARE TAKES THE VEIL

On July 16, 1193, Clare was born in Assisi, the daughter of Favarone di Offreduccio, a nobleman, and his wife Ortolana. She grew up in a well-to-do household and learned Latin, which was highly unusual for a woman in those days. At the age of fifteen, she refused to marry a nobleman who had asked for her hand since, as she confessed to her amazed parents, she had consecrated herself to God. In 1212, the day after Palm Sunday, she ran away from her father's home and, accompanied by her nurse, Bona di Guelfuccio, she went to the Portiuncola where Francis was waiting for her, as Bishop Guido was well aware.

Clare took off her precious garments and jewelry and donned a rough tunic that she tied around her waist with a cord. Francis cut her blonde hair and covered her head with a black veil. She took her vows of poverty, chastity and obedience, recognizing Francis as her superior. This marked the beginning of the Order of the Poor Clares.

THE MEETING OF FRANCIS AND CLARE AT THE PORTIUNCOLA

Clare, accompanied by Sister Pacifica, went to the Portiuncola to meet Francis and to see the dear church in which she had been consecrated to God. It was evening and the bread of charity was placed on a mat. The two saints began to discuss the Lord's redemptive sacrifice and his love for all creatures. Together, they lifted their voices in prayer to the Lord and were rapt in ecstasy. A heavenly light enveloped them and it was so intense that it seemed as if the woods around the church were ablaze. People came running from all over to put out the flames, but there was no fire, just a brother and sister in prayer.

THE SERMON TO THE BIRDS

Near Bevagna, he encountered a bevy of birds of a variety of species that were roosting in the trees or feeding in the fields. He rushed towards them and, treating them as if they had the faculty of reason, greeted them courteously. When he was in their midst, he zealous exhorted them to be quiet and to listen to the word of God: "My sister birds, you have good reason to praise the Lord. He has covered you with feathers and given you wings to fly, he has given you the air and gives you food so that you do not have to work for it." As he spoke, with a miraculous show of affection the birds stretched their necks, spread their wings, opened their beaks and observed him attentively. Lastly, he made the sign of the cross and blessed them all. The birds joyfully flew together through the air singing (Id. 12,3).

PAX ET BONUM!
Francis brought peace to many cities that were divided by bitter fighting between opposing factions. This happened in Assisi, Arezzo, Bologna and many other districts throughout Italy.

THE SPRING

Every time Francis quenched his thirst at a natural spring, he expressed his joy over God's precious gift of water, without which life could not exist. With his arms outspread and his eyes turned towards heaven, he voiced his feelings: "Praise be to Thee, my Lord, for Sister Water. She is useful and humble, precious and pure" (Canticle of the Creatures).

ST FRANCIS MEETS ST DOMINIC

St Francis and St Dominic, founders of the two most important monastic orders of the late Middle Ages, met and fraternally embraced each other during the Fourth Lateran Council.

The positive reforms of the Church, which were established during this Council and were codified by a papal bull issued by Innocent III, were largely the fruit of Franciscan and Dominican participation.

FAITHFUL TO POVERTY

One time it happened that on Easter, the brothers of the hermitage at Greccio prepared the table with more care than usual, but Francis did not approve. "He put on his head the hat belonging to a poor man who was present, he sat down on the ground and asked for a ladle that was set among the ashes.

"'Yes! Now I'm seated like a Friar Minor,' he said. 'We, more than anyone else, must feel ourselves obliged to follow the example of poverty set by the son of God'" (Little Flowers, Chap. 31).

BEFORE THE SULTAN OF EGYPT
VISITING JERUSALEM

In 1219, after the Crusaders had been vanquished during the Battle of Damietta in Egypt, as Francis was marching towards Jerusalem he was arrested, beaten and led before the Sultan, Melek-el-Kamel. The Sultan interrogated him at length and, once he

had verified his dauntless faith, he even grew to admire him. He offered him gifts (still preserved in the museum of the Basilica of St Francis) and gave him safe conduct to the Holy Sepulcher. During his visit to the Holy City, St Francis was overcome with emotion and prostrated himself in prayer.

THE THIRD ORDER

Francis' preaching stirred great religious fervor in men and women, making them want to follow in his footsteps. However, the duties, commitments and bonds in their lives were an obstacle. And yet, each person has his own vocation and his own place in the complex structure of society: everyone is useful and necessary in his place, in a harmonious blend of tasks, work and responsibility. Francis was a mystic, but he knew how to make the most of earthly and human realities in a concrete way. There is nothing to prevent anyone who works honestly throughout his life from observing the Gospel, whatever the form may be.

Therefore, with a fortuitous flash of intuition, "he decided to set up the Third Order, for everyone's universal well-being" (Little Flowers, Chap. XVI).

Lay people of any position, job or class who desire to join the Third Order are given the cord of obedience as their investiture.

THE WOLF OF GUBBIO

As recounted in the Little Flowers, in Gubbio there appeared a ravenous and ferocious wolf that killed animals and even people, so that everyone was afraid to leave the house. Francis met him, made the sign of the cross over him and said, "Come here, brother wolf. In the name of Christ, I order you not to hurt anyone." The wolf drew up to him and lay down at Francis' feet. The saint continued, "Brother wolf, you have killed God's creatures and done great harm for no reason.... I want you, Brother Wolf, to make peace between you and them, so they will not be harmed by you any more and so that they will forgive you."

The wolf accepted this peace proposal and indicated his willingness by gesturing with his head, ears and tail. Then he place his front paw in Francis' hands as a sign of faith. After that, the wolf continued to live in Gubbio for two more years. He went into the people's homes and never harmed anyone, nor did anyone hurt him."

THE RULE

The Rule, which was submitted to the General Chapter of the Friars Minor for their approval, was finally passed on November 29, 1223. This represents the way of life of the Order based on the teachings of the Gospel. It was dictated to Brother Caesar of Spyre, a profound expert on the holy scriptures, between the years 1221-1222 at the convent of Fonte Colombo in the Rieti Valley. This picture illustrates an important moment in the life of St Francis. The ministers of the Order, including Brother Elias, had asked Francis make the Rule concerning observance of the vow of absolute poverty less harsh. Francis, who was in love with Lady Poverty, was divinely inspired to reject this request decisively and, with an imperious gesture (surely the only time in his life),he declared in a strong voice, "This rule must be observed to the letter, without gloss, without gloss, without gloss."

CHRISTMAS AT GRECCIO

In 1223, Francis celebrated Christmas at Greccio in an unusual but highly poetic way.

He reproduced the scene of Jesus' birth in a realistic and three-dimensional form.

With the help of his friend, John Velita, he placed a hay-filled manger in the middle of a rocky gorge at the convent, and brought in live cattle and donkeys to stand alongside it.

He thus made a realistic reconstruction of the Nativity scene so that the

faithful could see "with their bodily eyes the hardship suffered by Baby Jesus."

"On Christmas Eve, friars, men and women, who had prepared candles and torches to light the way, came joyfully from all parts of the Rieti Valley.... The solemnities of the Mass were celebrated.... The saint of God was clothed with a deacon's vestments, for he was a deacon, and he sang the holy Gospel in a sonorous voice. And he preached to the people and spoke charming words about the nativity of the poor King."

BROTHER LEO'S MASS

Brother Leo entered the Order in 1209, immediately after the Rule had been approved.

He was such a meek, simple and pure priest that Francis named him "Brother Lamb".

He immediately became Francis' inseparable companion, acting as his confessor and secretary. In this role, he collected Francis' writings and made note of the special events in his life (the little flower on "perfect happiness" is well known). He was the first one to see Francis' stigmata, which he washed and took care of in strict secrecy. During his prayer and penance retreats, Francis listened to Brother Leo's recital of Holy Mass. Towards the end of his life, the Saint hand wrote a wonderful blessing on a small sheet of parchment especially for Brother Leo.

THE ANGEL AND THE VIOLA

In 1213, Francis did penance in the grotto of Speco di Sant'Ubaldo in Narni, which is a harsh, solitary and rocky place. While he was there, he became seriously ill and was afflicted with sharp pains. One night, an angel came down from heaven and, standing before his hovel on top of a natural rock column, comforted him with a celestial melody.

THE STIGMATA

Two years before his death, Francis stayed in the hermitage at La Verna. He was praying in ecstasy in a rough and rocky gorge when he saw a Seraph with six resplendent wings descend from heaven.

When he saw this vision, the Saint was amazed and was overcome with joy that was mixed with pain.

When the vision was over, he had bloody wounds on his hands, feet and side. "In fact, in five parts of his body the venerable father was marked with the sign of the passion and of the cross, as if he had been crucified together with the Son of God" (I Cel., 90).

THE BLESSING OF ASSISI

At the end of September in 1226, after he had been told by his doctor, John Buono of Marangone, that he was close to death, he lifted his arms up towards heaven and exclaimed, "Welcome, Sister Death!"

Then he immediately asked to be brought to his beloved Portiuncola, because he wanted to die in the place where he had first discovered the way of the truth and where he had founded his order.

He was placed upon a stretcher and carried towards the Portiuncola. He asked his brothers to stop at the foot of the hill, to lift him up and — since he was blind by this time —to turn him so he would be facing his city. As he was lovingly being supported by his brothers, he raised his arm as a sign of blessing and said, "Holy city, may God bless you, since because of you many souls will be saved, and many servants of God will live in you, and from you many will be chosen for the kingdom of eternal life. Peace be to you!"

DEATH

The year was 1226, and the date was Saturday, October 3rd, after sunset:
Francis was waiting for Sister Death to come.

He said to his brothers, "When you see that I am brought to my last mo-
ments, place me naked upon the ground and let me lie there after I am
dead for the length of time it takes to walk a mile unhurriedly" (II Cel.,
217).

Then, when there had gathered about many brothers, whose father and

leader he was, and while they were standing reverently at his side awaiting his blessed death and happy end, his most holy soul was freed from his body and received into the abyss of light and his body fell asleep in the Lord" (I Cel., 110).

"The larks came to the roof of the house and flew about it for a long time amid a great clamor. whether to show their joy or their sadness, we do not know" (Celano, Treatise).

CLARE'S FAREWELL

On the morning of Sunday, October 4, 1226, following the sacred funeral rites, a triumphal cortege accompanied the body of St Francis from his beloved Portiuncola to the Church of St George in Assisi, which would later become the site of the Basilica of St Clare.

The cortege made a detour from the normal route in order to give the